A History of Britain

INVADERS AND SETTLERS

450–1066

Richard Dargie

FRANKLIN WATTS

LONDON • SYDNEY

First published in 2008 by Franklin Watts

© 2008 Arcturus Publishing Limited

Franklin Watts
338 Euston Road
London NW1 3BH

Franklin Watts Australia
Level 17/207 Kent Street, Sydney, NSW 2000

Produced by Arcturus Publishing Limited,
26/27 Bickels Yard, 151–153 Bermondsey Street, London SE1 3HA

The right of Richard Dargie to be identified as the author of this work has been asserted by him in accordance with the Copyright, Designs and Patents Act 1988.

Series concept: Alex Woolf
Editor and picture researcher: Patience Coster
Designer: Phipps Design

Picture credits:
akg-images: 5, cover and 29 (Erich Lessing).
Ancient Art & Architecture Collection: 27 (R Sheridan).
Corbis: 6 (Leonard de Selva), 7 (Adam Woolfitt/Robert Harding World Imagery), 12 (Patrick Ward), 13 (Stapleton Collection), cover and 14 (Homer Sykes), 16 (The Mariners' Museum), 26.
Mary Evans Picture Library: 20, 23 (Mary Evans/Edwin Wallace), 25.
The Bridgeman Art Library: 8 (Lady Lever Art Gallery, National Museums Liverpool), 15 (© Look and Learn), 18, cover and 19 (British Museum, London, UK), 24, 28 (Victoria & Albert Museum, London, UK).
Topfoto: 11 (Doug Houghton).

Every attempt has been made to clear copyright. Should there be any inadvertent omission, please apply to the publisher for rectification.

A CIP catalogue record for this book is available from the British Library.

Dewey Decimal Classification Number: 941.01

ISBN 978 0 7496 8194 4

Printed in China

Franklin Watts is a division of Hachette Children's Books.

Contents

Germanic Invaders

Germanic troops had long served in Britain as Roman soldiers. After 450, however, Germanic peoples began to settle in southern Britain, creating new kingdoms and a new English culture.

Across the Narrow Water

The Angles, Saxons and Jutes were tribes that came from the coasts of north-west Germany and Denmark. Warriors from this region had raided the coasts of Gaul for many years. However, in 420 northern Gaul was settled by the powerful Franks. Forced out of Gaul, the Germanic tribes looked across the North Sea to Britain for plunder and new land. Over time, new settlers from Angeln near Kiel (a town in what is today Germany) gave their name to Angleland, or England.

The Coming of the Saxons

As their old nickname 'Dark Ages' suggests, little is known about the years after the end of Roman rule in Britain. Few written sources survive from the period. Much of what we know comes from a book called *The Ruin of Britain*, written in 540 by a monk called Gildas. He told of Gurthigern, or Vortigern, a chieftain who ruled the Britons of south-eastern England and hired Saxon warriors to fight for him. The first three Saxon ships, called *cyuls*, or keels, filled with Germanic warriors, landed in 449, and many others soon followed. Later legends told of the Jutish warlords Hengist and Horsa quarrelling with Gurthigern over pay and inviting their kinsfolk in Europe to join them in the conquest of the disorganized Britons. Defeated by the Jutes in 457, the Britons abandoned the area of Kent to the invaders. As Angles and Saxons poured into southern and eastern Britain, the native British were forced to leave the towns and the rich lowlands for poorer land in the north and west.

The Ruin of Britain

Gildas was a priest who believed that God was angry with the British and sent the Saxons as a punishment. Gildas' description of the coming of the Saxons was dramatic: 'High towers tumbled into the middle of the streets. Stones of high walls, holy altars, fragments of corpses, covered with bright clots of congealed blood - all crushed together and left unburied except in the ruins of houses, or in the ravening bellies of wild beasts and birds.'

Change and Continuity

Archaeologists believe that far fewer Anglo-Saxons migrated to Britain than was once thought. German and Briton often lived alongside each other, though probably in separate villages. Evidence from graves tells us that the local British survived and only adopted the customs of the invaders very gradually. Historians used to think that the Saxons murdered most of the British, but modern genetic evidence tells us that this did not happen.

The British chieftain Gurthigern welcomed the Saxons as allies, a decision that eventually led to his downfall.

Timeline

440s	• First Germanic settlements in southern Britain
457	• Saxon victory over the British at Crayford, Kent
540	• Gildas writes *The Ruin of Britain*

British Resistance

In Kent and Sussex, new Anglo-Saxon kings ruled over the native Britons. But British kingdoms survived in the west and north well into the 8th century.

Plague and Famine

After 450, several outbreaks of plague weakened the British population. The climate in Britain also became cooler and wetter at this time, making it difficult to grow crops in higher upland areas. This affected the British more than the new Germanic settlers, as the Britons' farms were often in the hillier lands in the north and west.

Arthur of the British – whether he existed or not – has the legendary reputation of a wise and just warrior king.

King Arthur

Ambrosius Aurelianus may be the source of inspiration for tales of Arthur, a Dark Age prince who successfully led the Britons against the invaders. Other Dark Age rulers linked to the myth of Arthur include Arthnou, a 6th-century warlord who may have built the fortress of Tintagel in Cornwall, and Artuir of the Scotii who lived near the old Roman fort of Camelon near Falkirk. These little-known figures inspired Geoffrey of Monmouth, a 12th-century priest, who wrote about the legendary Arthur in his fanciful *History of the Kings of Britain*.

Saxon Defeat

After the shock of the first Saxon invasions in the 450s, the British soon fought back. Ambrosius Aurelianus was a British leader who organized the people of Wiltshire and Somerset and won victories against the Saxons. He inflicted a heavy defeat upon the Saxons in 500 at the Battle of Mons Badonicus, or Badon Hill, near Bath.

British Strongholds

By 550, Tintagel in Cornwall and South Cadbury in Somerset were important centres of British power. These settlements were strong military forts, but they were also trading posts with links along the Atlantic coast of Europe to the Mediterranean beyond. Rheged in Cumbria was probably the homeland of King Urien, whose victories over the Saxons are celebrated in the Welsh *Book of Taliesin*. York remained in British hands until 580. The men of Gododdin, a kingdom in the Lothians, are remembered in an early Welsh poem that tells of their journey to meet heroic deaths in the Battle of Catterick in 600. The kingdom of Alt Cluth in central Scotland, later known as Strathclyde, was independent until the 8th century. Some Britons also migrated to Europe, founding Brittany in north-west France and possibly Galicia in Spain.

Many people believe that the settlement of Tintagel on the Atlantic coast of Cornwall was the birthplace of King Arthur.

British Survival

Historians used to think that the Britons were wiped out by the Germanic invaders, but modern writers now believe that in many areas of southern Britain the British and Saxon peoples slowly merged over time. In 8th-century Wessex, the British *wealas*, or Welsh, still lived alongside their Saxon rulers. Natives and invaders gradually created a new identity – as 'English'.

Timeline

440	• The climate cools across northern Europe
460	• British migration to Gaul increases
473	• Large Saxon forces arrive in Sussex
500	• Traditional date of the Battle of Badon Hill
550	• British power concentrated in western counties
600	• Gododdin warriors meet their deaths in the Battle of Catreath (Catterick)

An Age of Saints

The new Anglo-Saxon kings were pagan, but the Christian faith survived in the British Isles. Christianity was strongest in the west of Britain, where Christian kings protected the monks of the Celtic Church.

Christian Survivors

In 440 there were many Christian believers throughout Britain. Holy places such as the tomb of St Alban were still respected. At the start of the Germanic invasions, however, many Christians fled to western Britain where the rulers shared their faith. But although some Christians were martyred, the pagan kings in the south-east usually tolerated the beliefs of their native subjects.

Pagan Rulers

The new Anglo-Saxon kings worshipped the old gods of their Germanic homelands, but we know very little about them. Only the four days of the week, named after the Saxon gods Tiw, Woden, Thunor and Frige, remind us of this period of pagan belief in England.

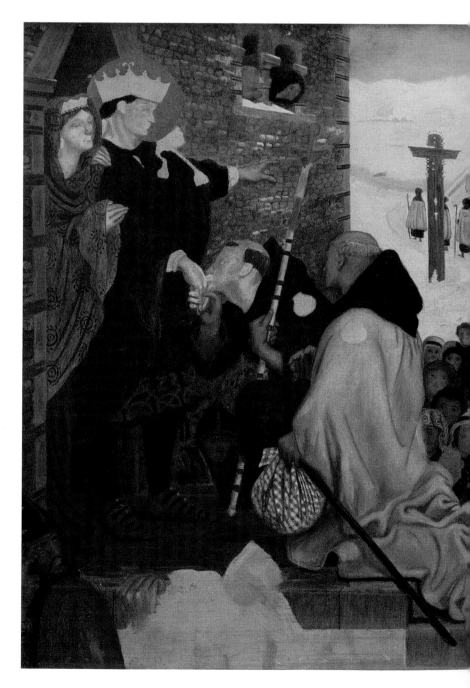

Missionary saints such as Aidan (shown here being received by Oswald of Northumbria) spread the Christian word throughout the kingdoms of Britain.

Missionary Saints

In 5th-century Ireland, the Romano-British missionary Patrick spread the Christian faith by founding monasteries and preaching to the High King of Ireland at his capital of Tara. St Columba was inspired by Patrick's example and founded an abbey on the Scottish island of Iona in 563. He preached to the northern Picts and, according to legend, defeated their druids in a trial of magic and calmed the great serpent of Loch Ness. In Wales, Dewi Sant or Saint David founded twelve monasteries with links to Devon, Cornwall, Brittany and Ireland. In the 7th century, missionaries from these western 'Celtic' abbeys set out to convert the English pagans. Celtic monks such as Aidan and Cuthbert worked among the Northumbrians, while St Chad preached to the Mercians of central England.

Roman Tradition

In 597, Pope Gregory in Rome sent the monk Augustine to England on a mission to convert the pagans of southern Britain to the Roman Catholic form of Christianity. King Ethelbert of Kent converted to Roman Catholicism in 601, but Augustine's mission to the Christians of western Britain was unsuccessful. They preferred their own Celtic ways of worship.

The Whitby Decision

Celtic and Catholic Christians held Easter on different dates. In Northumbria, King Oswiu celebrated the Celtic Easter, while his southern wife observed the Roman Catholic date. As a result, no one knew when to fast or when to feast. In 664, a synod (meeting) of church leaders was held at Whitby. Oswiu settled on the Roman date. Although he respected the Celtic St Columba, Oswiu feared being turned away from Paradise by St Peter of Rome. So the Roman Church became the main church in England. The Celtic Church was limited to its homelands in the west, the north and Ireland.

The date of Easter was finally agreed upon at the Synod of Whitby, held at Saint Hilda's Abbey (above) in today's Yorkshire.

Timeline

432	• Traditional date of Patrick's ministry in Ireland
560	• Dewi Sant establishes monasteries in Wales and Cornwall
563	• Columba arrives in western Scotland
597	• Arrival of Augustine in England
601	• Ethelbert of Kent is converted by Augustine
664	• Synod of Whitby chooses the Roman date for Easter

New Kingdoms

After the Roman Age, new local kingdoms grew up across the British and Irish isles. Some of these kingdoms were pagan and some were Christian. All were led by warrior kings who fought for land and power.

The Rule of Seven Kings

During the 6th and 7th centuries, a succession of kings won and lost power in England. Later, medieval historians tidied up the confusion of Dark Age England into a neat pattern of seven local kingdoms. This heptarchy, or rule of seven kings, was made up of Kent, Essex, Sussex, Wessex, East Anglia, Mercia and Northumbria. However, there were other 'lost kingdoms' that were not remembered by the historians. The kingdom of Lindsey, between the River Humber and the Wash, had moments of glory before it was defeated by Northumbria. The Hwicce kings ruled much of Worcestershire and Gloucestershire between 670 and 780. Other long-forgotten tribes of England include the Wihtware, who gave their name to the Isle of Wight.

Maps of England in the early Middle Ages show seven kingdoms, each ruled by its own monarch.

The British Kingdoms of Wales

In the 6th century, the Welsh nobles created new kingdoms such as Dyfed, Powys and Gwynedd. In the 630s Cadwallon, King of Gwynedd,

Fergus Mor Mac Earca

Like most Dark Age warlords, almost nothing is known about Fergus Mor Mac Earca, King of the Scotii. Fergus appears in early king lists and an early Irish writer records him as 'holding part of Britain' in 501. He probably ruled a small part of Argyll from the rock-fortress of Dunadd, the first 'capital' of the Scots. Fergus only became important much later, when medieval writers traced the line of Scottish monarchs back to him. With the union of the Scottish and English crowns in 1603, Fergus became the earliest identifiable historical ancestor of the British monarch.

won important victories over the Mercians and the Northumbrians. These halted the westward migration of the Anglo-Saxons for a century. Over time, however, the Welsh were forced back by Anglo-Saxon numbers and lost their more fertile lowlands.

Kingdoms in the North

In western Scotland, the British kingdom of Strathclyde grew up around the impregnable fortress of Dumbarton Rock that rose out of the River Clyde. Much of northern Scotland beyond the River Tay was occupied by Picts. In the far west, however, the people of Dal Riata in Argyll were Gaels who shared many cultural links with their cousins in Ireland, a short sea passage away. It used to be thought that the Dal Riata, later known as the Scotii, had migrated from Ireland to Kintyre. Modern archaeologists no longer believe this, but the people who lived in the southern Hebrides, a world of small islands and seaways, had many contacts with the Irish.

The natural fortress of Dumbarton Rock was the strategic and military centre of the kingdom of Strathclyde.

Northumbrian Glory

The Northumbrians were an energetic people from Angeln in Germany, who dominated northern Britain in the Dark Ages. They were powerful warriors and highly skilled in the arts.

Aethelfrith, Founding Father

Around 500, Germanic settlers founded two small kingdoms, Bernicia and Deira, on the north-eastern coast of England. The warlord Aethelfrith took Bernicia in 592 and Deira in 604, and became the founder king of Northumbria. The first English historian, Bede, described Aethelfrith as the first great king of the English, who 'conquered more British lands, expelling them and settling his own people, than any other king of the English'. Aethelfrith also defeated Scottish, Welsh and Mercian armies, making Northumbria the leading power in northern Britain.

The monastery at Lindisfarne in Northumbria was one of the great centres of Christian learning. The monks founded the first known school in the region, where reading, writing and Latin were taught.

Northern Expansion

In the 630s, the Northumbrians looked north to the rich farmlands of southern Scotland. King Oswald absorbed the eastern kingdom of Gododdin as far as the Firth of Forth and made inroads into the western British kingdoms of Rheged and Strathclyde. By the time of his death in 642, Oswald's kingdom included much of southern Scotland and most of northern England. The only threat that remained was the central English kingdom of Mercia. Oswald died fighting the Mercians, but his successor defeated them in the 650s. For a few brief decades, the Northumbrians were the masters of almost all of Britain.

Nechtansmere

Northumbria's fall was almost as quick as its rise. The kingdom was weakened by Mercian rebellions in the 650s and by a deadly plague in 664. In 685, King Ecgfrith marched against the Picts who lived in northern Scotland. Ecgfrith was greedy for slaves and plunder and he ignored his more cautious advisers. The Picts lured the Northumbrian army northwards, then ambushed them at the Battle of Nechtansmere in the Pictish heartlands of Angus. Ecgfrith and his nobles were massacred. Their destruction is commemorated on the great carved stone of Aberlemno which tells the story of the war. Pictish success at Nechtansmere made sure that the southern kings would not easily subdue the far north of Britain. Northumbrian military power was crushed, and it never recovered.

Golden Northumbria

A Christian kingdom after 627, Northumbria was deeply influenced by Celtic missionaries from Ireland and the north. Among these was St Aidan from Iona, who built a monastery at Lindisfarne near the royal fortress of Bamburgh. The artistic brilliance of the Northumbrians can be seen in the Lindisfarne Gospels, an illuminated manuscript produced around 715 that mixed Celtic and Anglo-Saxon artistic traditions. Another monastery, at Wearmouth, was famed throughout Europe for its collection of books. At nearby Jarrow, Bede wrote the first history of the English people.

A page from the magnificent Lindisfarne Gospels, illuminated manuscripts that combine the Celtic and Anglo-Saxon traditions.

Timeline

449	• Union of Bernicia and Deira
616	• Aethelfrith defeats the Welsh
655	• Oswiu defeats the Mercians
685	• Northumbrian nobles massacred at Nechtansmere
715	• The Lindisfarne Gospels are produced
731	• Bede writes his *Ecclesiastical History of the English People*

Dark Age Wales

In the 6th century, the British kingdoms in the north and west were separated from each other as the Anglo-Saxons penetrated into their lands. In Wales, a new sense of identity developed, based on language and different religious traditions.

The Westward Retreat

In the 6th century, there were strong links between the peoples of Wales and their British allies in other parts of the island. The poet Taliesin was bard to Welsh and Cumbrian princes. In the 7th century, a Welsh speaker in southern Scotland wrote the epic poem *Y Gododdin*. These bonds weakened as the Anglo-Saxons pushed westwards. The Saxon victory at Deorham in Gloucestershire in 577 drove a wedge between the Welsh and the Cornish when Gloucester and Bath were lost. The old Britons were increasingly pushed back into Wales.

Offa's Dyke (Clawdd Offa)

In 785, King Offa of Mercia ordered the building of a huge earthwork barrier between Powys in Wales and Anglo-Saxon England. The barrier, or dyke, was designed to prevent attacks on low-lying Mercian farmlands that had once been Welsh. In places it measured over 25 m (82 ft) in width and 8 m (26 ft) in height. Although it was soon abandoned, Offa's Dyke marked the frontier between Celtic and Saxon Britain.

The ditch and earth banks that formed the barrier of Offa's Dyke are still clearly visible in places today.

Welsh Kingdoms

Dark Age Wales was divided into a number of small states. The most powerful was Gwynedd in the north-west. Under its Christian King Cadwallon, the army of Gwynedd was strong enough to defeat the Northumbrians near Doncaster in 633. The principality of Powys in central Wales was less fortunate. In the 7th century, kings of Powys fell in battle against the Northumbrians. In the 8th century, Powys had to face the well-organized Mercians. By the 820s, this Welsh kingdom was exhausted by decades of warfare and much of its land was taken by its enemies.

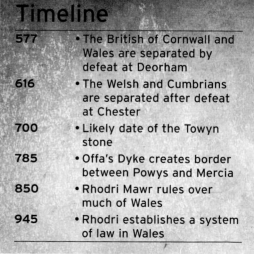

Language and Identity

The earliest known inscription in Welsh is on the Towyn stone in Gwynedd, carved around 700. The Welsh called themselves Cymry, or fellow countrymen. They had their own local form of worship. As in Ireland, hermitages and monasteries were places of spiritual power, where Welsh saints such as Asaph, Canna and Tydfil were honoured.

Rhodri Mawr

Rhodri Mawr, the Great, was the first High King of all Wales. Rhodri ruled Gwynedd in 844, but inherited other small kingdoms through marriage and good fortune. This made him ruler of much of Wales. His son, Cadell, added the lands of Dyfed to the kingdom. Rhodri's grandson, Hywel Dda, the Good, was a skilful and patient ruler who set down the laws of Wales and produced his own coinage. However, on his death in 950 his kingdom was split up into three smaller princedoms.

King Offa of Mercia oversaw the construction of Offa's Dyke. He hoped that it would protect the low-lying farmlands to the west of his kingdom.

Timeline

577	• The British of Cornwall and Wales are separated by defeat at Deorham
616	• The Welsh and Cumbrians are separated after defeat at Chester
700	• Likely date of the Towyn stone
785	• Offa's Dyke creates border between Powys and Mercia
850	• Rhodri Mawr rules over much of Wales
945	• Rhodri establishes a system of law in Wales

The Picts and Scots of Alba

*After 500, several tribes of people lived in Scotland.
Pictish kings ruled in the north. The Gaels or Scotii
ruled in the west. The British kingdom of Strathclyde
survived, despite attacks from the Norse and English.*

*A Pictish woman,
ready for battle:
down the ages the
Picts have often
been shown as
fierce, elaborately
painted warriors.*

The Picts

By the year 600 Pictish kings ruled northern Scotland, including
the fertile north-east area that was able to support a large
population. Although warlike, the Picts were successful farmers
and skilled craftsmen who used a written script known as
Ogam. At first pagan, the Picts became Christian in the
7th century. Their great fortress at Burghead in
Morayshire was protected on three sides by the sea and
on the fourth by a series of high ramparts and ditches.

Painted People?

We do not know what the Picts called
themselves. The word Picti appears in
a 3rd-century Latin poem and early
historians believed it stood for 'painted
people'. Modern scholars believe that
the name probably comes from an old
Celtic word, pett or pit, meaning a
piece of land. 'Pit' survives in many
place names in the old Pictish areas of
Angus, Aberdeenshire and Fife (for
example Pitcaple, Pitlessie). Norse
chroniclers called the tribes of
northern Scotland the Pehtas or Pettar.
Perhaps these ancient words are an
echo of the name that the Picts used
for themselves.

16

The Kingdom of Alba

In 750, the Picts ruled most of Scotland. A hundred years later their kingdoms had vanished. By the early 8th century, the Norse occupied large parts of northern Scotland that had once been Pictish. The Picts also had to deal with pressure from the Gaels of Dal Riata who were pushing eastwards to get away from Viking attacks on the coast. Historians used to think that the Pictish kings were wiped out in battle in the 830s. The Scottish king Kenneth MacAlpin marched into Pictland and forced the leaderless Picts to accept him as their ruler in 843. However, modern scholars believe that Kenneth MacAlpin had blood ties to both peoples and was the ideal leader for their common struggle against the Norse. The new united kingdom of Picts and Scots was called Alba, though its Latin name of Scotia became more common over time.

Constantine II

One of the most successful of the Alban kings was Constantine II, who ruled from 903 to 943. Despite setbacks, such as losing to the English at Brunanburh in 937, Constantine steered a careful course between the threats from the Norse and the English. Early in his reign he inflicted a serious defeat upon the Norse, clearing them out of fertile Strathearn. Later he allied himself with Viking rulers in York and Dublin, against the English. His careful diplomacy helped him to recapture the long-lost Lothians.

Frequent Viking attacks on the Atlantic coast forced the people of Dal Riata to move inland, where they clashed with the Picts.

Timeline

300	• First mention of the Picts by the Romans
500	• The Scots found Dal Riata, in Argyll
600	• Northern Scotland under Pictish control
685	• Picts defeat Northumbria at Battle of Nechtansmere
795	• Arrival of the Norse threat
830s	• Norse control large parts of Pictland
843	• Union of the Picts and Scots under Kenneth MacAlpin
930s	• Constantine II's alliance with Viking York helps Scots recapture the Lothians

Dark Age Culture

Historians used to call the years after 500 the 'Dark Ages' because they thought they were brutal and primitive. Modern scholars believe instead that this was an age of great learning and culture.

The Light of Faith and Learning

Throughout Britain, 'Dark Age' Christians were busy building abbeys, churches, libraries and schools. The great abbeys at Iona (563), Lindisfarne (635) and Jarrow (674) were places where monks studied as well as prayed. Here they created masterpieces such as the illuminated Gospels, begun at Iona but transferred for safety in the Viking age to Kells in Ireland. Much of what we know about Britain in this period flowed from the pens of monks such as Bede and Nennius, author of the *Historia Britonum*. Caedmon, the earliest known English poet, wrote his verse at Whitby Abbey in the 600s.

Courts and Culture

Kings also encouraged learning and the arts. Edwin and Oswald of Northumbria replaced the first wooden minster at York with a stone structure in the 630s to show their piety and their wealth. Alfred of Wessex built abbeys and schools and even went back to school himself when he was an adult. To make sure he was remembered after his death, Alfred asked the Welsh monk Asser to write down his life story. As a result, we know far more about Alfred than any other Dark Age prince.

Bede, a Northumbrian monk living in the 7th and 8th centuries, is best known for his history writings.

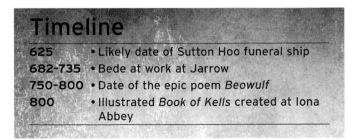

Timeline

625	• Likely date of Sutton Hoo funeral ship
682–735	• Bede at work at Jarrow
750–800	• Date of the epic poem *Beowulf*
800	• Illustrated *Book of Kells* created at Iona Abbey

Beowulf

The Old English epic poem *Beowulf* is typical of the tales enjoyed by Saxon warriors. The hero Beowulf overcomes the monster Grendel to win honour and becomes King of the Geats, a Scandinavian people. In old age, Beowulf takes up his sword again to fight a great dragon, but is slain in the moment of victory. His people lay out their beloved chieftain on a great ship 'covered in many treasures and ornaments from far off lands, a vessel fitted out with weapons of war and a host of treasures to travel far with him into the power of the flood'. The 8th-century poet describes the exact scene that was revealed by archaeologists' discovery of a ship at Sutton Hoo (see below).

An iron and gilt bronze helmet found at the Sutton Hoo funeral ship site in Suffolk shows the influence of Germanic and Scandinavian cultures on designs of the time.

Warrior Culture

The discovery of a 7th-century royal funeral ship at Sutton Hoo in Suffolk gives us a glimpse of the life of a Dark Age king. The 28-metre-long ship was laden with fabulous treasure, armour and weapons that show the fine skills of Saxon artists and craftsmen. Much of the treasure was decorated with scenes from the pagan myths of Scandinavia. Spoons engraved with the names Saulos and Paulos and silver bowls marked with the Cross hint at wider links to the Christian lands of southern Europe.

19

The Warrior Kings of England

Thanks to their successes against the Danes, the kings of Wessex emerged as the leaders of 'English' resistance against the Vikings. Wessex was lucky to have several energetic rulers who strengthened their realm and even dreamed of ruling all Britain.

Alfred the Great

Alfred's victory at Edington in 878 gave Wessex some valuable time to prepare itself for the struggle against the Danes. Alfred used the peace that followed to strengthen his kingdom by building *burhs*, or fortified settlements, to protect every important place in Wessex. While some men served in the *fyrd*, or militia, others were sent home to rest and tend their farms. Alfred also built a strong fleet of ships that helped him stop further warbands of Danes landing on the coasts of southern England. Before his death in 899, Alfred, the only English monarch known as 'Great', had recaptured London and added the old kingdoms of West Mercia and Kent to his realm.

Alfred of Wessex, known as 'the Great', held out against the Danes and expanded his realm across Kent and Mercia.

Timeline

871	• Winchester becomes capital of Wessex
886	• Boundary of the Danelaw established by Alfred and Guthrum
915	• Alfred's son Edward restores the Danelaw to English rule
930	• Border between Cornwall and England established at the River Tamar
937	• Athelstan wins the bloody Battle of Brunanburh
950s	• Kings of Wessex recapture much of northern England

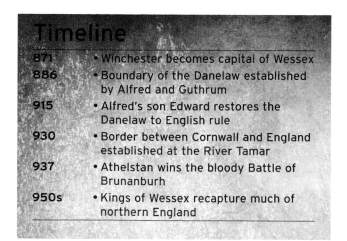

Children of Alfred

Alfred's children continued his work. Edward used the title 'King of Angles and Saxons' to show that he fought for all the English. He built fortresses at key points such as Stafford and pushed the Danes north of the River Humber. Alfred's daughter Æthelflaed survived a kidnap attempt by the Danes and ruled from Stafford for eight years, recapturing Derby and Leicester.

Athelstan

Athelstan was a bold and successful soldier who pushed the borders of his realm almost to those of modern England. Within three years, he had seized back York and absorbed Northumbria into his kingdom. In the far west he pushed the independent Cornish back beyond the River Tamar. Athelstan also pressed his father's claim to be the overlord of all Britain. Documents from his court called him *rex totius Britanniae*, King of all Britain, a claim that was resented by the independent Welsh and Scots.

The Secret of Wessex Success

The Wessex kings ruled in a way that made sure their commands were carried out. Officials in the shires (ealdormen, shire-reeves and hundredmen) served the king and were rewarded with grants of land and titles. Strong laws and taxes made sure that Wessex could always put a well-armed militia into battle.

Brunanburh

In 937, the Scots, Cumbrians, Irish and Norse joined together in an alliance against Wessex. They feared the land-grabbing ambitions of Athelstan, the English king. The two sides met at the bloody Battle of Brunanburh, in which many kings and nobles were slaughtered. According to one Irish writer, 'a multitude of Saxons fell but Athelstan obtained a great victory'. Athelstan died a year after the battle, but his success against the alliance made sure that Anglo-Saxon England survived.

Athelstan's army was victorious at Brunanburh, one of the bloodiest battles of the age.

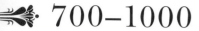

Life in Anglo-Saxon England

A way of life grew up in Anglo-Saxon England that was based on the old customs of the Germanic tribes. Anglo-Saxons generally lived in simply built homes in small towns that were close to their centres of agriculture.

Saxon Buildings

Most Anglo-Saxon houses were built around a frame of wooden posts with walls of wattle and daub or wooden planks, topped with a thatched roof. Many were built above a sunken pit or basement, which was filled with straw in the winter to insulate the room above. Even the houses of rich nobles were built in this simple way and had just one main room with an earthen or wooden floor. There would be a hole in the roof to allow the smoke from the hearth to escape. Over time, these buildings were burned down or rotted away, so none of them survives today. Some Anglo-Saxon churches do survive because they were built in stone. The Saxons also raised huge, finely decorated stone crosses to mark holy places or where main roads met.

Thanes, Ceorls and Slaves

There were two classes of freeman in Anglo-Saxon England – thanes and ceorls. Some thanes were wealthy noblemen with vast estates, while others were modest landowners. Ceorls, or churls, were the poorest freemen who owned just enough land to feed their families on the main crops of oats, barley, peas, lentils and beans. There were also many slaves in England at this time. Some were children born into slavery or sold by their parents, while others were adult prisoners taken in battle. Slaves could buy their freedom if their family could meet the price demanded by the slave's owner.

Saxon stone-carving decorates a font in a church in Dorset, England.

Anglo-Saxon Women

Men were much more important than women in Anglo-Saxon England, but women did have some rights. Although marriages were arranged between families, a woman could not be married to a man against her wishes. She could own her own land and property and keep control of it even when she married. If her husband treated her badly in any way, she could seek justice and compensation from him. Women from noble families were often well educated and many helped their husbands to govern their estates and households.

Anglo-Saxon noblewomen wore tunics (one is shown here with an embroidered hem) and veils.

Rough Justice

The early Anglo-Saxons had simple ways of punishing criminals. Thieves and burglars had their fingers or hands removed. If a man was murdered, his relatives had the right to avenge him by killing someone from the murderer's family. This led to long and bloody feuds between families, so a system of *wergeld*, or fines, was set up. A convicted murderer had to pay *wergeld* based on the social rank of his victim. A thane was worth 1,200 shillings, but the family of a ceorl only received compensation of 200 shillings. A slave was worth about 50 shillings.

Scandinavian England

By 1000, Scottish kings and Irish princes had managed to deal with the Viking threat. However, England suffered new attacks from the Danes after 980, and even became part of a Danish North Sea empire.

King Sweyn of Denmark launched repeated revenge attacks against England after the St Brice's Day massacre of Danish settlers in 1002 (see opposite).

False Calm

By 980, the Scottish kings of Alba had learned how to deal with the Vikings. A band of Norse warriors who landed on the shores of Argyll in 986 were immediately rounded up and hanged. Scottish King Malcolm II destroyed a Danish host at Mortlach in Morayshire in 1010. The Irish leader Brian Boru captured the Norse bases of Limerick and Dublin in the 960s, before breaking the power of the Irish Vikings forever in the great slaughter at Clontarf in 1014. However, England fell completely under Scandinavian control in the early 11th century.

Maldon

In 991, a Danish army of 4,000 defeated a smaller English militia on the banks of the River Blackwater at Maldon in Essex. An Anglo-Saxon poem about the battle tells us about Byrhtnoth, a heroic Essex ealdorman who chose to die in battle rather than surrender. Despite this brave act, the English King Aethelred decided not to follow suit. Instead he 'bought off' the invaders with money payments known as Danegeld.

Danegeld

After Maldon, Aethelred handed over 4,500 kg (10,000 lbs) of silver to the Danes 'on account of the great terror that they caused'. Sweyn Forkbeard, King of Denmark, was persuaded to call off his siege of London in 994 thanks to a similar bribe. However, Aethelred soon found he had to make more payments to the Danes in 1007, and again in 1012. Over 60 million silver pennies were given to the Danes between 990 and 1016, yet chroniclers still complained that 'the Danes went about England as they pleased'.

The St Brice's Day Massacre

In 1002, Aethelred ordered the murder of all Danes in England. On St Brice's Day (13 November) most of the Danish nobles in England were massacred. However, rather than solving Aethelred's problems, the killings angered King Sweyn, who launched revenge attacks upon England. Aethelred fled to Normandy and in 1017 Sweyn's son, Cnut, became King of England.

Scandinavian Rule

In the course of his nineteen-year reign, Cnut also became King of Denmark and Norway. England was just one part of his empire. Cnut ruled his English subjects fairly; he confirmed the laws of the English and was generous to the Church. His new coinage helped the recovery of English trade with Europe after years of difficulties. Following Cnut's death in 1035, his sons Harold Harefoot and Harthacnut each reigned for only a short time. Viking invasions in 1066 and 1075 were unsuccessful. The Viking age in England was over.

King Cnut and his queen: the son of Sweyn Forkbeard, Cnut ruled as King of England for nineteen years.

Timeline

991	• Danish victory at Maldon in Essex
991	• Aethelred buys off the Danes with 4,500 kg of silver
1002	• St Brice's Day massacre of Danish nobles in England
1003-13	• Revenge invasions of England by Danes
1013	• Aethelred flees to Normandy
1017	• Cnut becomes King of England
1035	• Death of King Cnut
1042	• England returns to Anglo-Saxon rule under Edward the Confessor

The Last of the Old Kings

By 1050, Scotland and England were becoming strong kingdoms. But uniting the separate princedoms of Wales would prove more difficult.

'King of the Welsh Britons'

In the 1050s, a powerful warlord united the separate Welsh princedoms under his rule. This was Gruffydd ap Llywelyn, who governed all Wales from his court at Rhuddlan and even won back the rich borderlands that had been lost to Mercia. However the 'greater Wales' that Gruffydd carefully put together quickly fell apart after his death in 1063.

Here Macbeth is shown as a character from Shakespeare's play of the same name. The fictional Macbeth was portrayed as an assassin goaded on to murder by his ambitious and ruthless wife, but the real Macbeth is believed to have been a popular, virtuous monarch.

Macbeth, King of Scots

Macbeth was a fierce warrior who won the crown by defeating King Duncan in battle in 1040. Macbeth's long and popular reign as king was largely peaceful. His wife Gruoch was a pious woman who gave much of her wealth to the Church. Together they travelled to Rome as pilgrims to give alms to the poor. Macbeth successfully resisted an English invasion of Scotland in 1054, but eventually died from his battle wounds in 1057.

From Alba to Scotland

The Gaelic kings of Alba were more successful at building a kingdom. At the Battle of Carham in 1018, Malcolm II won back the lands north of the Rivers Tweed and Solway, including the Lothians. The old divisions between Pict and Scot faded. In each part of Alba, a *mormaer*, or local noble, ran his district for the king, giving him soldiers and support in times of crisis. Most importantly, only three kings ruled Alba for most of the 11th century, and this gave the kingdom order and stability.

The Last Anglo-Saxon Kings

By the 11th century, England was the richest and most powerful kingdom in the British and Irish isles. King Edward the Confessor had grown up in Normandy in France and he encouraged trade and other links with Europe. He also invited Norman nobles to help him run England. Saxon nobles resented this and there were riots and rebellions against the king and his Norman friends in the 1050s. For the last three years of his life, Edward was under the control of Harold Godwinson, a brilliant soldier and Earl of Wessex. When Edward died in early 1066 without an heir, Harold was his natural successor as he controlled several rich earldoms and had experience in war and government. In January 1066, Godwinson was crowned Harold II.

The Building of Nations

Between 500 and 1050, waves of invaders had settled in the British Isles. Most of these peoples were absorbed into the kingdoms of Scotland and England that gradually emerged from decades of war. The peoples of these kingdoms were loyal to one king, and had a growing sense of themselves as either Scots or English.

The reign of Edward the Confessor, King of England from 1042–66, saw a gradual loss of royal control. This embroidered image of the king is from the Bayeux Tapestry.

Timeline	
1018	• Scottish victory at Carham secures the Tweed-Solway border
1040-57	• Rule of Macbeth of Alba
1042	• Edward the Confessor becomes King of England
1060	• The high point of Gruffydd ap Llywelyn's rule in Wales
1063	• Harold Godwinson becomes strongest figure in England
1066	• Death of the childless Edward the Confessor on 4 January
1066	• Godwinson crowned as Harold II on 5 January

Glossary

archaeologists people who study the past through the scientific analysis of remains such as buildings, artefacts and bones

bard a poet to a prince

besiege to surround a place with troops

Celtic based on the customs of the old tribes of Britain and especially Scotland, Wales and Ireland

compensation money paid to someone who has been wronged

convert to try to make someone join your church or faith

culture the ways of life and customs of a people

diplomacy making alliances or friendships with other countries against your enemies

druids the priests of the old religion of the Welsh and the Picts

earldom estate or lands owned by an earl

earldormen local government officials who were in charge of shires

epic a long story or poem, usually about heroes and great deeds

Gaels a Celtic people

Gaul the Roman name for France

hermitage a place where holy men go to pray alone to God

hundredmen local government officials who were in charge of the hundreds (divisions of the shires)

identity a sense of belonging to a particular tribe, people or nation

impregnable well defended and protected

independent having to obey no higher king or power

insulate to protect from cold or heat

kinsfolk relatives or family

loot to steal wealth and goods

migration the movement of people from one land to another

militia army made up of part-time soldiers

ministry the work of a religious leader

minster a large church or cathedral

missionary a priest who travels to a land to convert the inhabitants to his faith

monastery a group of buildings where priests live, work and pray together

Norse people from Norway or Scandinavia

pagan believing in the old gods of the ancient Britons; also describes a person who holds religious beliefs that are not those of the world's main religions

Picts the people of northern Scotland

plunder wealth and goods stolen by force

rampart the wall of a fort, often made from earth and wooden stakes

sack to steal goods from and destroy

Scandinavia the Viking homelands of Norway, Sweden and Denmark

Scotii the Roman name for a tribe of people from Scotland

shilling an old silver coin worth twelve pennies

shire-reeves royal officers in charge of local government (the word *sheriff* comes from 'shire-reeve')

wattle and daub a mixture used for building walls, usually made of twigs woven together and plastered with clay, lime, water and sometimes dung and straw

Timeline

440s	• First Germanic migrants settle in southern Britain
500	• Victory of the western British over Saxons at Badon Hill
501	• Fergus King of Scots – earliest ancestor of the present monarch
560s	• Columba and David build abbeys and schools in Scotland and Wales
597	• Arrival of Augustine at Canterbury
604	• Kingdom of Northumbria founded by union of Bernicia and Deira
660	• High point of Northumbrian power
664	• Synod of Whitby chooses the Catholic form of Christianity
685	• Picts defeat Northumbrians at Battle of Nechtansmere
730	• Bede writes first history of the English people
785	• Offa of Mercia builds a dyke on the Welsh border
790s	• First raids by Danish and Norse Vikings
800	• *Book of Kells* begun at Iona Abbey
843	• Union of Picts and Scots under Kenneth MacAlpin
850	• Rhodri the Great rules over almost all Wales
878	• Creation of the Viking Danelaw in north-eastern England
937	• Athelstan wins Battle of Brunanburh, but at great cost
950	• Most of England under the rule of the Wessex kings
991	• Aethelred pays Danegeld of 4,500 kg of silver
1002	• Massacre of the Danes in England
1017	• Danish Cnut becomes King of England
1018	• Border between Scotland and England settled by Battle of Carham
1066	• Deaths of the last Anglo-Saxon kings of England

Further Information

Books

Anglo-Saxon and Viking Britain, Alex Woolf, Franklin Watts, 2006

Alfred the Great, Andrew Matthews, Franklin Watts, 2002

Viking Times, Fiona Corbridge, Franklin Watts, 2006

Scotland in the Middle Ages 400-1450, Richard Dargie, Pulse Publications, 2001

Websites

www.postroman.info/
an excellent site with a wide range of articles, lists and maps relating to many aspects of life in all parts of Dark Ages Britain, including Scotland and Wales

www.bbc.co.uk/history/ancient/anglo-saxons/
very informative site on most aspects of Anglo-Saxon England, with an emphasis on culture, language and identity, and with links to games and interactive pages for schools

http://saxons.etrusia.co.uk
website that covers most aspects of life in Anglo-Saxon England in a clear manner

www.britannia.com/history/saxontime
timeline for Anglo-Saxon England with detailed descriptions of key events

Index